RACHEL WHITEREAD

RACHEL WHITEREAD

Plaster Sculptures

LUHRING AUGUSTINE GALLERY
KARSTEN SCHUBERT LTD

A STRANGE FAMILIARITY

EACH OF RACHEL WHITEREAD'S PLASTER WORKS IS DIRECT, CLEAR AND LITERAL: a trace of specified objects in a pale, inert cast. They have an unornamented, uncluttered appearance, something common to much contemporary sculpture. The materials and means of execution are declared unambiguously on the surface of the work. But for all its directness of means, this sculpture offers little of the immediacy of impact which characterises much recent work. This sculpture is elusive, ambiguous, and figural. It leaves a sense of something being held back, of something virtual and not quite there, something the viewer will have to work for to find. Its mode is not confrontational but quiet. It takes time to look at, and time to consider the consequences of this looking. It can't be taken in at a glance. It is, so to speak, slow sculpture.

'Yellow Leaf' (1989), the first work by Whiteread I saw, in January 1990, had something of the look of minimalist sculpture about it: slab-like, apparently abstract, almost regular, almost monochrome. Almost, but not quite. There were nagging discrepancies. The monolithic plaster shapes weren't quite regular enough, the surfaces not quite smooth or clean enough and a section of laminated wood was embedded flush with its upper surface. But these minimalist 'failings' turned out to be clues. The laminate rectangle in 'Yellow Leaf' was the middle section of a kitchen table top, and once this reference was registered it became clear that the blocks of plaster were themselves descriptive in some way. But it took time to see that these forms were themselves cast directly from a table. In this case the internal divisions and upper surfaces of the blocks carried the imprints of the physical structure of the table, whereas the outer vertical surfaces were determined by an imaginary plumbline dropped from the table edge. What was being described then was not a table so much as a volume of space below it, represented as a solid block.

The next work I saw, 'Cell' (1990), was taller and thinner, but essentially a similar block-like construction. By this time of course I was expecting to read the surface detail as a negative imprint of some thing. But it still took a while to calculate exactly what it was I was looking at. In time I recognised that the object I was puzzling over was again absurdly familiar – a simple fireplace with tiled surround, typical of almost every cheap late-nine-teenth-century or early-twentieth-century domestic interior. 'Cell' hinted at what 'Ghost' (1990) established beyond doubt: that there was far more to Whiteread's sculptures than a clever device. 'Cell' already looked a more confident work. Simpler and more concise than 'Yellow Leaf' (there were no sections of the actual object embedded in the plaster), it was also stranger. This has something to do with the way the viewer is positioned by the work. The point at which the fireplace is seen in the work is also the point at which the viewer sees that he or she is looking at it from an impossible or a fictional position – behind it. Through the looking glass. And yet the work is so literal, so un-fictional, a direct trace of a specific object, down to the soot-marks in the grate.

'Cell' leads to 'Ghost'. This remarkable centrepiece of the plaster works was first exhibited during the early summer of 1990 at the Chisenhale Gallery in east London. Where previously we had seen casts taken from the furniture of unremarkable domestic interiors, here was the entire interior space itself made physical. And here again the viewer has to take on some of the identity of Alice to participate in this work. Once more we have to learn to see cavities as protrusions – a smooth black hole as a door handle, a series of circular depressions as a light switch, the negatives of skirting-board and picture-rail – and protrusions as the cavities of a sash-window, a door and a fireplace. In this way, moving around the work and inspecting the details, we gradually build up a picture of something very familiar – a living room. Something so familiar we would never normally spend much time or attention looking at it. And once more we have to see ourselves viewing the 'room' from an impossible standpoint.

The dignified mute form of 'Ghost' now looks like the inevitable development of Whiteread's experiments in casting. But to have the idea of casting an entire room is one thing, to execute it quite another. First there is the practical problem of finding an appropriate site – Whiteread always picks her subjects with great care. Eventually she chose a room in a Victorian terrace in Archway, north London. Then there are the many predictable and unpredictable problems concerning the materials, construction processes, time, money, helpers and friends needed to realise this kind of ambitious project. But 'Ghost' looks magnificent so we quickly forget about the determination, patience and trouble that went into making it.

'Ghost' remains Whiteread's largest work to date. After 'Ghost' there is a period of consolidation and fine tuning. In particular there are two clusters of work. One group is cast from the undersides of sinks and baths, while the other is derived from beds and their bases. A particularly noticeable feature of sinks and baths is that each imprint is contained within a larger overall form, the shape and size of which is entirely independent of the cast object. This is further emphasised by the fact that each of these blocks situates its negative imprint significantly higher than it would be found in normal use. In these works Whiteread stresses the independence of the finished sculpture from the object which was originally cast. This may have been necessary for Whiteread after the highly mimetic 'Ghost' – in which all the visible faces were determined by the space from which it was cast. But even here numerous decisions had to be made which were not just determined by the technical issues of casting. For example, Whiteread spent several days prior to casting the living-room planning exactly what size and shape the individual plaster sections should be – considerations which are at least as much æsthetic as they are practical. In all these sculptures the selection of an object and the casting of it are stages in the production of another object. They are points of departure. The finished sculpture is a thing in its own right, independent of and never simply reducible to its ostensible starting point.

The mattresses and bed bases from 1988–91 appear rather more naturalistic. The floor-based work from this series, 'Untitled (Bed)' (1991), is beautifully simple and austere: two identical shallow blocks punctuated by a small round hole at each corner: the space beneath an ordinary double bed. But the sculptural mass doesn't correspond to the actual space under a normal bed – at over twelve inches it is too high. The depth of the work is a quality of the sculpture but was not a property of the bed. Likewise the two vertically placed works from this series, 'Untitled (Yellow Bed, Two Parts)' (1991) and 'Untitled (Freestanding Bed)' (1991), record the shabby unseen undersides of beds, but only in one plane. In certain respects these works have as much in common with painting as sculpture: a wall of plaster acts as the equivalent of the wooden stretcher to support a flat frontal surface where the picturing takes place. (Like a number of sculptors of recent years Whiteread originally trained as a painter.)

In another way Whiteread's three-dimensional work is related to that other medium of two-dimensional representation: photography. Clearly the technical processes of casting are firmly rooted in the traditions of the sculptor's studio. But as with photography, casting's relationship with its original is indexical rather than autographic. Each represents by leaving a trace of one material upon another – of light on a photochemical surface, or of an object on a quick setting fluid. The process is closer to transfer than to translation. And in each certain properties are transferred while others are omitted. Whiteread's sculptures are in this sense monochrome monotone negatives – utterly faithful to and yet at the same time utterly unlike the objects from which they are derived.

After 'Ghost' few doubted the seriousness of Whiteread's sculpture and many became fascinated by its strange, virtual character. This has led inexorably to bouts of interpretation. In conversation Whiteread has discussed the material aspects of her production and has also touched on her sense of its existential and emotional character. This latter side comes in part from her choice of subjects. Domestic, inexpensive, mass produced and marked by use, these items could easily form the unseen backdrops in dozens of family snapshots. And for Whiteread the choice of subject is strongly influenced by its capacity to trigger certain kinds of memory and association. Memories, not so much of the particular objects she grew up beside, but of the kinds of spaces – under a table or a bed, inside a wardrobe – which are the intimate and exclusive habitats of childhood. Or associations, especially in the earlier work, with particular people or events.

But these very personal kinds of association are not available to the viewer simply from looking at the work – although a sense of it being emotionally charged in some way may be. Nor is it easy for the viewer imaginatively to inhabit the kinds of spaces represented in the plaster. It isn't always possible to retrace the steps made by the artist, as the viewer only starts when the work is finished. We don't see a table or a living room, but an opaque chunk of space marked out by a trace of its container. It is at least as much a sense of alienation from the object as proximity to it which marks out the viewer's psychological position. But it is an intriguing kind of alienation. It impedes perception. Slows it down. The viewer is made to take note of that which is normally passed over. We begin to scrutinise what is usually registered automatically, if at all – the mouldings on a door frame, the weave on the underside of a bed, and so on. In beginning to break down the habits of perception the transparent is made opaque. The familiar, in the phrase of the Russian Formalist critic Victor Schlovsky, is made strange. Above all we become alienated from our habits of perception – and in the process more aware of them.

Objects are usually static and silent but these sculptures are still and quiet. It's an effect which has often been noticed and is usually attributed to the encased and tomb-like appearance of the work. This is certainly a factor but only part of the story. The mood of a work is a complex thing, something vividly experienced but hard to pin down. Some of the stillness we experience when looking at Whiteread's sculpture comes from the material she uses. Plaster has a different kind of inertness from, say, stone or metal. It appears to be light and brittle (which it isn't particularly) and thus to require great care to be taken of it, even when being looked at. Its pallor adds to its unassertive quality. Imagine 'Ghost' cast in iron, and how that might imply a different way of approaching and moving round the sculpture. (Alternatively, imagine a Richard Serra cast in plaster.) Some other sense of the stillness of Whiteread's work comes, I think, from the effect described earlier, of having our perception impeded, of slowing down and intensifying the processes of looking. This is not the same as stillness by association, it is more a psychological condition of looking at these objects. And such careful looking requires or implies a kind of quietness. In another way these sculptures are still in that each work is 'a still' in the photographic sense. The sculptures isolate an object from its cycle of use, disuse, exchange and re-use. They fix a moment in the passage of an object through time. This effect is made all the more intense by Whiteread's choice of objects which bear the traces of extensive wear. They have a sense of duration inscribed in them in a way that a new bed or a showroom bath does not. But it is only in their being removed from circulation, only in being stilled, and then distilled into sculpture, that it becomes possible really to look – and to see the strange in the familiar.

DAVID BATCHELOR

PLATES

MANTLE 1988
plaster and glass
24" x 47 1/4" x 20 7/8"
Collection the Artist

CLOSET 1988
wood, felt and plaster
63" x 34 5/8" x 15 3/8"
Collection the Artist

SHALLOW BREATH 1988
plaster and polystyrene
75 1/4" x 36 5/8" x 7 1/8"
Collection the Artist

These three sculptures and TORSO 1988 (illustrated on page 44) formed
Rachel Whiteread's first one-person exhibition at the Carlile Gallery in London, 1988

YELLOW LEAF 1989
plaster, formica and wood
37" x 59" x 29"
Collection Calouste
Gulbenkian Foundation

FORT 1989
plaster and wood
35 1/2" x 51 1/4" x 29 1/8"
Private Collection, London

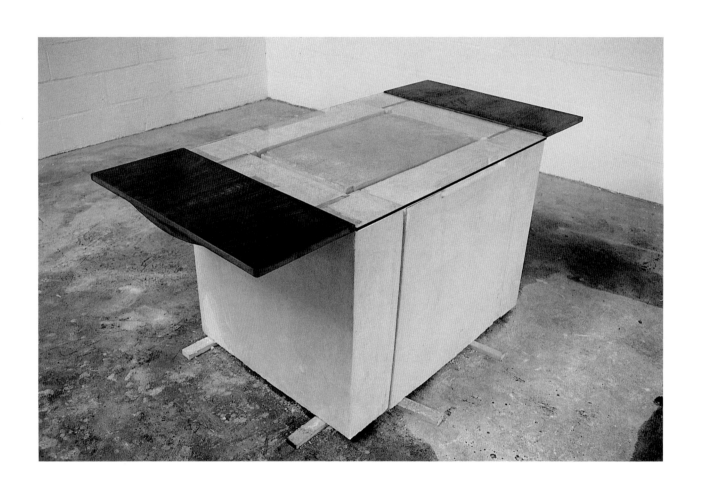

LEDGER 1989
plaster, wood and glass
30 7/8" x 67" x 38 3/8"
Collection Richard Salmon,
London
(studio installation)

FLAP 1989
plaster and wood
29 1/8" x 36" x 29 1/2"
Private Collection
(studio installation)

CELL 1990
plaster
48 1/2" x 49 1/2" x 20 1/2"
Private Collection, Belgium
Courtesy Laure Genillard
Gallery, London
above: work in progress

GHOST 1990
plaster on steel frame
106" x 140" x 125"
Saatchi Collection, London

GHOST 1990
plaster on steel frame
106" x 140" x 125"
Saatchi Collection, London

ETHER 1990
plaster
43" x 34 $^1/_2$" x 80"
Collection Jay Jopling, London
(studio installation)

UNTITLED (SQUARE SINK) 1990
plaster
42" x 40" x 34"
Saatchi Collection, London
(studio installation)

VALLEY 1990
plaster and glass
37 $^1/_2$" x 73" x 38"
Stedelijk Van-Abbemuseum,
Eindhoven
(studio installation)

FALSE DOOR 1990
plaster
84 ¹/₂" x 60" x 16"
Collection British Council, London
(studio installation: front and back)

UNTITLED (BATH) 1990
plaster and glass
40 $^1/_2$" x 41 $^1/_2$" x 82 $^1/_2$"
Saatchi Collection, London

UNTITLED (BED) 1991
plaster
12" X 74" X 54"
Collection Doris Lockhart,
London
(studio installation)

UNTITLED (YELLOW BED,
TWO PARTS) 1991
dental plaster
66" x 27" x 14"
Private Collection, Courtesy
Luhring Augustine Gallery,
New York

UNTITLED (FREESTANDING
BED) 1991
dental plaster and polystyrene
41" x 72" x 9"
Southampton City Art Gallery

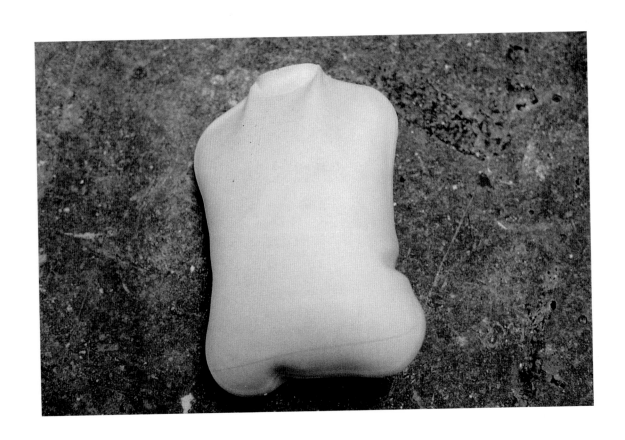

TORSO 1988
plaster
3 1/2" x 10 5/8" x 6 3/4"
Private Collection, London

UNTITLED (TORSO) 1991
dental plaster
4 1/2" x 11" x 7"
Private Collection, Courtesy
Karsten Schubert Ltd, London

UNTITLED (TORSO) 1992
dental plaster
3" x 9" x 6 1/2"
multiple, edition of 12 + III

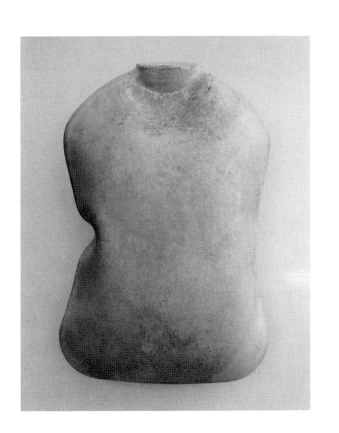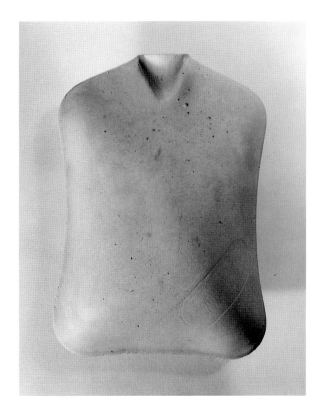

UNTITLED (FLOOR) 1992
plaster
9 $1/2$" x 110 $1/2$" x 245"
Karsten Schubert Ltd, London

UNTITLED (AIR BED) 1992
plaster and polystyrene
8 5/8" x 47 1/4" x 76 3/8"
Karsten Schubert Ltd

UNTITLED (PLATFORM) 1992
plaster and polysterene
11″ x 61 3/4″ x 128 3/8″
Galerie Claire Burrus, Paris
(studio installation)

RACHEL WHITEREAD

Biography and bibliography

Born: 20th April 1963, London
lives and works in London and Berlin

EDUCATION:

1982-85 Brighton Polytechnic
1985-87 Slade School of Art UCL

ONE-PERSON EXHIBITIONS:

1988 Carlile Gallery, London
1990 'Ghost', Chisenhale Gallery, London
1991 Arnolfini Gallery, Bristol
     Karsten Schubert Ltd, London
1992 'Rachel Whiteread: Recent Sculpture', Luhring Augustine
     Gallery, New York
     'Rachel Whiteread: Sculptures', Centre Cultural, Fundacion
     Caja Pensiones, Barcelona
     'Rachel Whiteread: Sculptures', Stedelijk Van-Abbemuseum,
     Eindhoven
1993 Galerie Claire Burrus, Paris
     'Rachel Whiteread: Zeichnungen', D A A D Galerie, Berlin

GROUP EXHIBITIONS:

1987 'Whitworth Young Contemporaries', Manchester
1988 'Riverside Open', London
     'Slaughterhouse Gallery', London
1989 'Concept 88 Reality 89', University of Essex Gallery
     'Whitechapel Open', London
1989 'Deichtorhallen', Hamburg
1990 'British Art Show', touring exhibition
     'A Group Show: Mat Collishaw, Hanne Darboven, Angus
     Fairhurst, Günther Förg, Michael Landy and Rachel
     Whiteread', Karsten Schubert Ltd, London
1991 'Marina Abramovic, Kate Blacker, Marie Bourget, Angela
     Bulloch, Leslie Foxcroft, Paola Pezzi, Tessa Robins, Kay
     Rosen, Yoko Terauchi, Marylin Weber, Rachel
     Whiteread', Victoria Miro Gallery, London
     'Metropolis', Martin-Gropius-Bau, Berlin
     'Kunst Europa', Kunstverein, Pforzheim
     'Broken English: Angela Bulloch, Ian Davenport, Anya
     Gallaccio, Damien Hirst, Gary Hume, Michael Landy,
     Sarah Staton and Rachel Whiteread', Serpentine
     Gallery, London
     'Katharina Fritsch, Robert Gober, Reinhard Mucha, Charles
     Ray and Rachel Whiteread', Luhring Augustine Gallery,
     New York
     'Turner Prize Exhibition: Ian Davenport, Anish Kapoor,

Fiona Rae and Rachel Whiteread', Tate Gallery, London
     'Confrontaciones '91', Palacio de Vélazquez, Madrid
1992 'Doubletake: Collective Memory and Current Art', Hayward
     Gallery, London
     Fifth Anniversary Exhibition, Karsten Schubert Ltd, London
     'Damien Hirst, John Greenwood, Alex Landrum, Langlands
     and Bell, and Rachel Whiteread', Saatchi Collection,
     London
     'Skulptur-Konzept: Carl Andre, Pedro Cabrita Reis, Tony
     Cragg, Dan Flavin, Donald Judd, Richard Long
     Wilhelm Mundt, Ulrich Ruckriem, Serge Spitzer, Rachel
     Whiteread', Galerie Ludwig, Krefeld
     'DOCUMENTA IX', Kassel
     'Contemporary Art Initiative: Contemporary Works of Art
     Bought With the Help of the National Art Collections
     Fund', Kiddell Gallery, Sotheby's, London
     'London Portfolio: Dominic Denis, Angus Fairhurst, Damien
     Hirst, Langlands and Bell, Michael Landy, Nicholas
     May, Marc Quinn, Marcus Taylor, Gavin Turk, Rachel
     Whiteread and Craig Wood', Karsten Schubert Ltd,
     London
     'Lili Dujourie, Jeanne Silverthorne, Pia Stadtbaumer, Rachel
     Whiteread', Christine Burgin Gallery, New York
     'Summer Group Show: Robert Barry, Keith Coventry, Angus
     Fairhurst, Michael Landy, Stephen Prina, Bridget Riley,
     Rachel Whiteread and Alison Wilding', Karsten Schubert
     Ltd, London
     'Lea Andrews, Keith Coventry, Anya Gallaccio, Liam Gillick,
     Damien Hirst, Gary Hume, Abigail Lane, Sarah Lucas,
     Steven Pippin, Marc Quinn, Marcus Taylor and Rachel
     Whiteread', Barbara Gladstone Gallery and
     SteinGladstone Gallery, New York (curated by Clarissa
     Dalrymple)
     'New Voices: Recent Works For the British Council
     Collection' (David Ausen, Keith Coventry, Ian
     Davenport, Jeffrey Dennis, Peter Doig, Gary Hume,
     Callum Innes, Elisabeth MacGill, Antoni Malinowski,
     Julian Opie, Fiona Rae, Michael Stubbs, Suzanne
     Treister, Alison Turnbull, Rachel Whiteread, Tony
     Cragg, Bill Woodrow, Anish Kapoor, Richard Deacon),
     Centre de Conference Albert Borschette, Brussels (and
     tour)
     '1992 Sydney Biennale', Sydney
1993 'Passageworks: Geneviève Cadieux, Lili Dujourie, Dan
     Graham, Asta Gröting, Gary Hill and Rachel
     Whiteread', Rooseum Centre for Contemporary Art,
     Malmö

PUBLICATIONS:

1989 'Concept '88 Reality '89', University of Essex Gallery
1990 Einleuchten-Deichtorhallen Hamburg (ill)
     'The British Art Show': touring exhibition (ill)

'Ghost': Chisenhale, London (ill)

1991 Andrew Renton and Liam Gillick: 'Technique Anglaise:
Current Trends in British Art', Thames and Hudson,
One-Off Press, London and New York (ill)

1991 Christos M Joachimides and Norman Rosenthal (eds):
'Metropolis', exhibition catalogue, Rizzoli International
Pulications Inc, New York (english edition) (ill)

Andrew Graham-Dixon: 'Broken English', exhibition catalogue, Serpentine Gallery, London (ill)

Sean Rainbird: 'The Turner Prize 1991', Tate Gallery
Publications 1991 (ill)

1992 Lynne Cooke, Bice Curriger and Greg Hilty (eds):
'Doubletake: Collective Memory and Current Art',
Parkett Verlag Zurich and South Bank Centre, London
(ill)

Sarah Kent: 'Young British Artists: John Greenwood,
Damien Hirst, Alex Landrum, Langlands & Bell and
Rachel Whiteread', The Saatchi Collection, London (ill)

Ramon Martinez de Velasco (ed): 'Confrontaciones: Arte
Ultimo Britanico y Espanol', Ministerio de Asuntos
Sociales and The British Council, Madrid (ill)

'Signes des Temps', Fondation BMW, Paris (ill)

'Silence: Contradictory Shapes of Truth', exhibition catalogue, Moderna Galerija Ljubljana (ill)

'Skulptur-Konzept', exhibition catalogue, Galerie
Ludwig,Krefeld (ill)

'DOCUMENTA IX', exhibition catalogue (3 vols), Edition
Cantz, Stuttgart and Abrams, New York 1992 (also
German edition) (ill)

'Rachel Whiteread: escultures', exhibition catalogue, Sala
Moncada de la Fundació "la Caixa", Barcelona

Liam Gillick, 'Lea Andrews, Keith Coventry, Anya Gallaccio,
Damien Hirst, Gary Hume, Abigail Lane, Sarah Lucas,
Steven Pippin, Marc Quinn, Marcus Taylor, Rachel
Whiteread', artist's book to accompany exhibition at
Barbara Gladstone and SteinGladstone, New York (ill)

Andrea Rose and Gill Hedley (eds): 'New Voices: New
Works For the British Council Collection', British
Council London (ill)

REVIEWS:

1990 Kate Bush: British Art Show, *Artscribe*, Spring, p 71 (ill)

Andrew Renton: 'Birth of the Cool', British Art Show, *Blitz
Magazine*, January, pp 54-55

William Feaver: British Art Show, *The Observer*, January

Liam Gillick: The British Art Show, *Art Monthly*, March

James Hall: 'Ghost', *Sunday Correspondent*, June 24, (ill)

William Feaver: 'Ghost'/British Art Show, *The Observer*, July 1

Andrew Graham-Dixon: 'Ghost', *The Independent*, July 3
(ill)

Richard Cork: The British Art Show, *The Listener*, July 5, p 42

Sarah Kent: 'Ghost', *Time Out Magazine*, July 11, (ill)

Giles Auty: British Art Show, *Art Line*, Vol 5, No 2, Summer,
pp 12-13

Sachiko Tamashike: 'Ghost', *Nikkei Art*, Japan, September,
p 143 (ill)

Andrew Renton: 'Ghost', *Flash Art*, October, Vol XXIII, No
154, pp 158-159 (ill)

Liz Brookes: Rachel Whiteread, Chisenhale, *Artscribe*,
Nov/Dec, No 84, p 80 (ill)

William Feaver: 'View down the Grant Aid Road', *The
Observer*, Dec 30

1991 Tim Hilton: 'Making Room For A Ghost', *The Guardian*, Jan 9

Linda Blampied: 'Sculptures provoke strange sensations',
Keynsham Weekly Chronicle, Jan 25

Rachel Whiteread at the Arnolfini Gallery, *Epigram
Magazine*, Feb 4

Rachel Whiteread at the Arnolfini Gallery Bristol, *Spike
Magazine*, February, No 188

Rachel Whiteread at the Arnolfini Gallery, Bristol, *Venue
Review*, Feb 15

Sasha Cradock: Rachel Whiteread, Karsten Schubert Ltd,
Critic's Choice, *The Guardian*, Feb 27

Patricia Bickers: Rachel Whiteread at the Arnolfini, Bristol,
and Karsten Schubert Ltd, London, *Art Monthly*, March,
No 144, pp 15-17

William Feaver: 'Stiff Upper Lip', *The Observer*, March 3

Sarah Kent: Rachel Whiteread, Karsten Schubert Ltd,
London, *Time Out Magazine*, March 13, No 1073 (ill)

Enrique Juncosa: Rachel Whiteread, Karsten Schubert Ltd,
Lapis Magazine, April, No 77, p 78 (ill)

Adrian Searle: 'Eleven Women Artists', *Time Out Magazine*,
April 24, No 1079, p 43

William Feaver: 'Metropolis', *The Observer*, April 28, p 57

Jurgen Hohmeyer: 'Manie der Blauen Laube: Die Berliner
Ausstellung Metropolis', *Der Spiegel*, April 29, No 18

Roberta Smith: 'A Show in Berlin That's All Over The Map',
The New York Times, May 5, p 37

Mary Ann Francis: 'Sculpture at Victoria Miro', *Art Monthly*,
May, No 146, p 21

James Hall: 'Global Village: Metropolis in Berlin', *The
Independent*, May 16

Alfred Nemeczek: 'Metropolis', *Art Kunstmagazin*, May, No
6/91, pp 54-62

Michael Archer: 'Ghost Meat: Michael Archer considers the
sculpture of Rachel Whiteread', *Artscribe*, June, No 87

David Galloway: ''Metropolis', Crossroads or Cul-de-Sac?'.
Art in America, July, pp 46ff

Marco Livingstone: 'L'heritage du pop art anglais leurres:
voir double', *Art Press*, July/Aug, No 160, pp 18ff (ill)

Iain Gale and Dalya Alberge: 'Youth and Beauty? The 1991
Turner Prize', *The Independent*, July 16, p 17 (ill)

Richard Dorment: 'A Prize Turnabout', *The Daily Telegraph*,
July 16, p 14 (ill)

Tom Lubbock: 'Shortlist short on ideas', *The Independent on*

Sunday, July 21, p 20

Bruce Bernard: 'Salvage From The Wreck', *The Independent Magazine*, Aug 3, pp 36-38

William Packer: 'The diminishing value of novelty', *Financial Times*, Aug 6, p 21

Brian Sewell: 'Putting on the zits', on 'Broken English', *Evening Standard*, Aug 8, p 21

Charles Hall: 'Tests of Raw Nerves', *The Sunday Times*, Aug 11, p V.10

Iain Gale: 'Broken English', *The Independent*, Aug 13, p 13 (ill)

Matthew Collings: 'New Contemporaries at the I C A and Broken English at the Serpentine Gallery', *City Limits Magazine*, Aug 15, No 515, p 18

Sarah Kent: 'Breaking Ground', *Time Out Magazine*, Aug 14, No 1095, p 39

Tim Hilton: 'Composition With Old Hat', *The Guardian*, Aug 14, p 30

Roberta Smith: 'Preview of upcoming season', *The New York Times*, Sept 8, p 49

Emma Dexter: Rachel Whiteread at the Arnolfini in Bristol and at Karsten Schubert Ltd, London, *Sculpture Magazine*, Sept/Oct, p 88 (ill)

Stuart Morgan: 'The Turner Prize', *Frieze Magazine*, Oct, No 1, pp 5/6 (ill), 9/10 (ill)

Kozue Watanabe: 'Metaphors and Visions in British Contemporary Art', *21st Century Prints*, Tokyo, Oct, p 131 (ill)

William Feaver: 'The Prize Fight', (British) *Vogue*, Nov, p 68

Brian Sewell: 'Mockerey nook', *The Evening Standard*, Nov 7, p 30

Richard Cork: 'Young, Gifted and Rising Too Fast?', *The Times*, Nov 8, p 14

Sarah Kent: 'Prize Fighters', *Time Out Magazine*, Nov 13, No 1108, p 23

Matthew Collings: 'The Turner Prize at the Tate Gallery and We've Lost E T But the Boy's Coming Back at Karsten Schubert Ltd', *City Limits Magazine*, Nov 21, No 529, p 18

Giles Auty: 'The Cringe Before the Binge', *The Spectator*, Nov 16, pp 57-58

William Feaver: 'Breaking the Mould: Sculptor Rachel Whiteread is a frontrunner for the Turner Prize. William Feaver discovers her cast-off world', *Observer Magazine*, Nov 24, pp 66-67 (ill)

Marjorie Allthorpe-Guyton: 'Made In Heaven: The 1991 Turner Prize', *Artscribe*, Nov/Dec, No 89, p 15

Andrew Graham-Dixon: 'Je m'accuse', *The Independent*, Nov 26, p 16 (ill)

Tim Hilton: 'The £ 20,000 game of charades', *The Guardian*, Nov 26, p 34

William Packer: 'The Changing Expectations of the Turner Prize', *The Financial Times*, Nov 26, p 19

Sean Rainbird: 'The Turner Prize 1991', *Patrons of New Art Newsletter*, Winter, No 14 p 2

David Lister: 'Art prize launched into illusory space', *The Independent*, Nov 27, p 6

Rory Knight Bruce and Brian Sewell: 'Lashings of Champagne and Streams of Consciousness', *Evening Standard*, Nov 27, p 1 and 19 (ill)

Louisa Buck: 'Rachel Whiteread's Space Craft', *Connoisseur Magazine*, Dec, Vol 221, No 959, p 109 (ill)

'The Returns on the Turner Prize', *Art Monthly*, Dec/Jan, No 152, p 2

1992 Geraldine Norman: 'Art For Art's Sake Not For Youth's Sake', *The Independent*, Jan 4, p 39 (ill)

Roberta Smith: 'Rachel Whiteread at Luhring Augustine Gallery', *The New York Times*, Jan 17, p C38

'Rachel Whiteread at Luhring Augustine', *The New Yorker*, Feb 10, p 12

Kay Larson: 'Of Dogs and Man', *New York Magazine*, Feb 10, Vol 25, No 6, pp 54/55

William Feaver: 'Once More With Feeling', *The Observer*, Feb 23, p 57

Louisa Buck: 'Buying British', (British) *GQ*, March, p 44

'Rogue's Gallery', *Elle Magazine*, March, p 88

'The Whiteread Prize', (British) *Vogue*, March, Vol 156, No 2325, p 25 (ill)

Michael Birt: 'Charlie Is Their Darling', *The Sunday Times Magazine*, March 8, pp 40-44 (ill)

William Feaver: 'A Jape With The Jaws of Death', *The Observer*, March 8

William Packer: 'From Dreams to Dead Fish', *The Financial Times*, March 10, p 19

Andrew Graham-Dixon: 'Great White Hopes', *The Independent*, March 10, p 18

Richard Dorment: 'Disturbing Symbols of Death', *The Daily Telegraph*, March 11, p 22

Liam Gillick: 'Doubletake', *Art Monthly Magazine*, March, No 154, p 14/15

Emmanuel Cooper: 'Pry Society: On Doubletake at the Hayward Gallery', *Time Out Magazine*, March 5, No 1124, p 36

Matthew Collings: 'Young British Art at the Saatchi Collection', *City Limits Magazine*, March 12, No 544, p18

Sacha Craddock: 'Schools of Small Fish in The Saatchi Pond', *The Guardian*, March 13

Roger Bevan: 'Saatchi Collection Opens Exhibition of Young British Art', *The Art Newspaper*, March 16

Mick Brown: 'Smart art of Making Nothing Happen', *The Daily Telegraph*, March 13, p 17

Emmanuel Cooper: 'Karsten Couch', *Time Out Magazine*, March 11, No 1125, p 39

Andrew Graham-Dixon: 'Great White Hopes: Young British Art At The Saatchi Collection', *The Independent*, March

10, p 18

David Lillington: 'Fishy Business: Young British Artists at the
Saatchi Collection', *Time Out Magazine*, March 18, No
1126, p 37

Andrew Wilson: 'Rachel Whiteread', *Forum International*,
March/April, Vol III, No 12, pp 78-80 (ill)

Richard Cork: 'Tanks for the memories: Young British artists
at the Saatchi Collection', *The Times* (Life & Times),
April 3, p 3

Ruth Barter: 'Doubletake', *Art Monthly Magazine*, April, No
155, pp 16-17

Stuart Morgan: 'Thanks for the Memories', *Frieze Magazine*,
April/May, pp 6-11

Ian Pendleton: 'Just When You Thought It Was Safe...',
Esquire Magazine, June, p 22

CVM: 'On The Road to Kassel', *Artforum Magazine*, June,
Vol XXX, No 10, pp 78-83 (ill)

Andrew Graham-Dixon: 'A marathon of mediocrity' (DOC-
UMENTA IX), *The Independent*, June 16, p 16

Roberta Smith: 'A Small Show Within an Enormous One',
The New York Times, June 22, p C13

Sarah Kent: 'Rachel Whiteread', *Modern Painters Magazine*,
Summer, Vol 5, No 2, pp 86/87 (ill)

James Hall: 'Young British Artists' (Saatchi Collection),
ARTnews Magazine, Summer, Vol 91, No 6, p 147

Robert Heller: 'Report on the 1991-1992 PNA Acquisitions
Sub-Commitee', *Patrons of New Art Newsletter*,
Summer, No 15 (ill)

Michael Archer: interview with Rachel Whiteread, *Audio
Arts*, August, Vol XII, No1

Robert Taplin: 'Rachel Whiteread at Luhring Augustine', *Art
in America Magazine*, Sept, p 124 (ill)

Stuart Morgan: 'Rachel Whiteread: la melancholie des
moulages', *Art Press Magazine*, Sept, No 172, pp 37-
40 (ill)

Ralph Rugoff: 'Dark Art', (American) *Vogue Magazine*, Sept,
pp 352-358 (ill)

'DOCUMENTA IX', *Audio Arts*, Sept, Vol 12, No 2 & 3

Philippe Braem: 'With Attitude', *The British Council/Philippe
Braem*, Brussels, Sept

Steven H Madoff: 'DOCUMENTA IX: More Is A Mess',
ARTnews Magazine, Sept, pp 129-131

Roberta Smith: 'A Young Group From Britain', *The New
York Times*, Oct 16

'Oh you Pretty Things...The Loss of the Goldsmiths Touch',
Casablanca Magazine, Oct, Vol 1, No 1, pp 24/25

Jutta Schenk-Sorge: 'Zwolf Junge Britische Kunstler: Stein
Gladstone und Barbara Gladstone Gallery, New York',
Kunstforum International, Nov, Vol 120, pp 397/398
(ill)

Peter Schjeldhal: 'Twelve British Artists at Barbara Gladstone
Gallery and Stein Gladstone New York', *Frieze
Magazine*, Dec, Issue 7, pp 45 (ill)

Carol Kino: 'Young British Artists' (Barbara Gladstone), *Art
& Antiques*, Dec, p 82

'Recent Acquisitions of twentieth-century sculpture by British
museums', *The Burlington Magazine*, Dec, pp 842- 846
(ill)

1993 'Pick of the Year', *Arts Review Magazine*, Jan, Vol XLV, pp
18/19 (ill)

1993 © David Batchelor, Karsten Schubert Ltd,
Luhring Augustine Gallery, Rachel Whiteread
Photographs:
Peter Cox, pp 24, 27; Alex Hartley, p 43;
Sue Ormerod, pp 25, 45; Gareth Winters, p 37;
Ed Woodman, pp 29, 31, 33, 34, 35, 47; Werner Zellien, pp 49, 51;
Courtesy Luhring Augustine Gallery, p 41;
Courtesy Karsten Schubert Ltd, pp 14, 15, 17, 19, 20, 21, 22, 39, 44;
Courtesy South Bank Centre, London, p 23

Edited and designed by Peter Chater
Set in Futura Book and Futura Demi
Printed by Pale Green Press, London,
in an edition of 800 copies
March 1993

ISBN 1 870590 20 1
(Karsten Schubert Ltd)

LUHRING AUGUSTINE GALLERY
130 Prince Street
New York, New York 10012
212-219 9600 FAX 212-966 1891

KARSTEN SCHUBERT LTD
85 Charlotte Street London W1P 1LB
071-631 0031 FAX 071-436 9255